To Celia
Merry Christmas
1998

love Dad

1998 | STAMP
YEARBOOK
UNITED STATES POSTAL SERVICE

32
USA

1998

BALLET

Table of Contents

Berlin Airlift delivers food and fuel in 1948-49 blockade

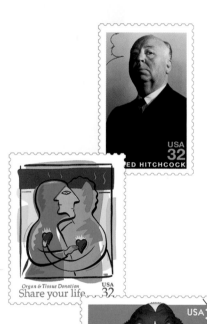

*Stamp issue dates and denominations reflect dates
and rates at press time.*

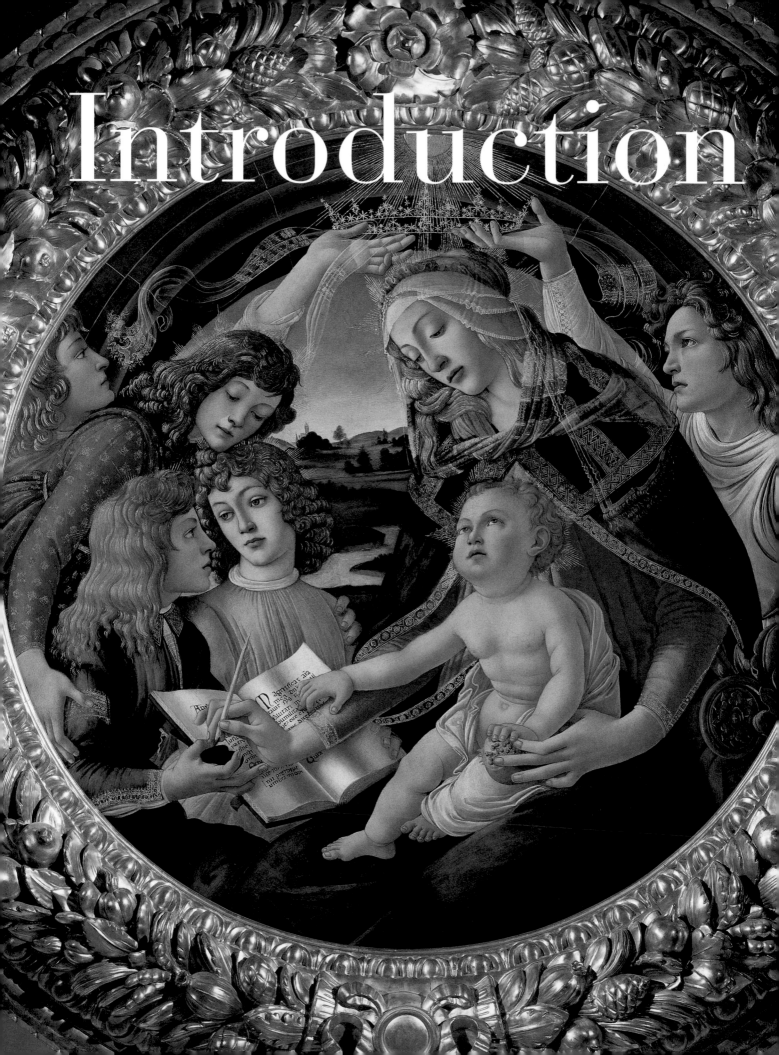

Introduction

A postage stamp may be small, but it faces an enormous challenge. Capturing the essence of a person, event, or issue in such a compact frame is a formidable task. Yet the images displayed in the United States Postal Service's *1998 Stamp Yearbook* not only meet this challenge, but do so with elegance and beauty.

From historic events to charitable causes, influential people to natural beauty, this year's collection depicts a genuine diversity of subjects. People of all ages and interests will undoubtedly find a stamp to cherish.

People who have contributed to American entertainment grace several of these stamps. Those honored range from Hollywood icons to musical talents. Alfred Hitchcock, the "Master of Suspense," and the popular duo of Sylvester and Tweety embody our nation's eclectic movie and television influences. Eight prominent American singers of the 20th century are also featured, representing both folk and gospel music. The performing arts are captured in a lovely image evoking the elegance of ballet.

American art is represented in several other stamps. Alexander Calder's kinetic sculpting genius and Stephen Vincent Benét's poetic power are featured, as 1998 marks the 100th anniversary of their births. A classic sheet covering four centuries of American masterpieces, as well as a stamp of an exquisite 15th-century *Madonna and Child* relief, are also spotlighted.

This year's commemorative compilation not only focuses on legendary figures, but on significant issues as well. Philanthropy is one such subject. A stamp honoring organ and tissue donation is also featured, emblematic of the spirit of giving and sharing. Tribute is also given to renowned African-American philanthropist, Madam C. J. Walker.

Defining moments in American history are prominent in the 1998 issuance. The centennial of the sinking of the U.S.S. *Maine* is observed, as are milestone anniversaries of the Berlin Airlift and Klondike Gold Rush. Indeed, these stamps are poignant reminders of both triumphant and tragic events in the country's past 100 years.

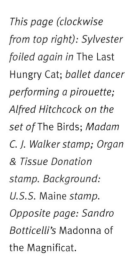

This page (clockwise from top right): Sylvester foiled again in The Last Hungry Cat; *ballet dancer performing a pirouette; Alfred Hitchcock on the set of* The Birds; *Madam C. J. Walker stamp; Organ & Tissue Donation stamp. Background: U.S.S.* Maine *stamp. Opposite page: Sandro Botticelli's* Madonna of the Magnificat.

The nation's natural panorama and wildlife are also represented with stamps displaying a variety of America's flowering trees and tropical birds. Wisconsin celebrates its 150th birthday with a depiction of the state's rural beauty. These images pay tribute to America's diverse landscape, showcasing examples from across the country.

Stamps portraying holidays bring a festive dimension to the collection. From Cinco de Mayo to the Lunar New Year, celebrations that transcend national and cultural boundaries are honored. Also featured are four stamps, each depicting a holiday wreath and each reflecting the seasonal spirit of a different region of the United States.

Along with the legendary figures and significant events, there are colorful stamps brimming with playfulness and imagination. A collection of bright-eyed critters is presented to animal lovers and pet owners of all ages. Equally vibrant is a futuristic out-of-this-world scene that reflects our infatuation with the exciting possibilities of outer space.

Highlighting the compilation is a truly special inclusion — a centennial reissue of the 1898 Trans-Mississippi series, featuring "Western Cattle in Storm," regarded by many to be the most beautiful stamp ever.

This page (clockwise from middle right): Wisconsin hills formed by glaciers; Chinese New Year dragon in Vancouver, British Columbia; colorful chili wreaths in Santa Fe, New Mexico; reissue of the celebrated stamp, "Western Cattle in Storm;" Lunar New Year stamp. Background: Cinco de Mayo stamp. Opposite page: girl captivated by a bright-eyed goldfish.

These are just brief overviews of the fascinating topics included here. The stamps offer powerful symbols of numerous subjects, many with equally captivating stories behind their images.

Whatever the subject, each stamp featured here is a small piece of America, a significant thread in our national fabric. The stamps should be admired for their ability to reveal the heart of so many American treasures. Indeed, the *1998 Stamp Yearbook* powerfully crystallizes the rich culture and history that has shaped our country.

Place
Stamp
Here

Lunar
New Year
Year of the Tiger

January 5, 1998 • Seattle, Washington

A traditional holiday of prosperity, the Lunar New Year remains one of Asia's most widely celebrated events. Each year, the festival honors one of the 12 animals of Chinese astrology. As 1998 marks the Year of the Tiger, it pays tribute to the mighty feline's courage and protective power. The U.S. Postal Service is pleased to commemorate the occasion with its sixth stamp in the Lunar New Year series, a special paper-cut design by a prominent Chinese-American artist.

Because the Chinese calendar is based on the rotation of the moon, rather than the solar months used in the Western world, the Lunar New Year begins in late January or early February. As such, the date is often called the Spring Festival and is welcomed throughout Asia with a sense of renewed spirit and confidence in the approaching year. Families and friends congregate, exchange presents, and set off firecrackers to ignite a holiday atmosphere.

*T*his year's tiger stamp is the latest in the Lunar New Year series to feature colorful illustrations of Chinese astrology animals done as paper cuts, a folk art still popular in China.

The concept of yin and yang—cosmic forces that balance the extreme elements of human nature—is the cornerstone of the 12-animal astrological cycle. This year's honored creature symbolizes bravery and the ability to drive off evil demons. For instance, those born in the Year of the Tiger are believed to share an optimistic and adventurous personality. But beware: The bold felines are also prone to volatile friendships and rash behavior.

Not all tigers are alike, however. The Chinese measure the passage of time in 60-year periods that are also influential. According to legend, "Tigers Standing Still" (those born in 1914 and 1974) are unusually cautious and reserved. On the other hand, "Tigers Passing Through the Forest" (1902, 1962) are wildly aggressive with stormy temperaments.

This page (clockwise from top right): three Sumatran tiger cubs; dragon dancers celebrating the Lunar New Year in New York City's Chinatown; a painted cloth tiger from China's Ch'ing dynasty. Opposite page: the tiger, a symbol of bravery and protection according to Chinese astrology.

11

Place
Stamp
Here

Winter Sports

January 22, 1998 • Salt Lake City, Utah

Each winter brings a unique spirit of athletic competition. Whether hitting the snowy slopes of international events or playing hockey on a local frozen pond, people in cold climates everywhere bear the elements and savor the thrill of winter sports.

Cold-weather sports have a surprisingly long history. A short wooden object discovered in Sweden—later determined to be a cross-country ski—is believed to be more than 4,500 years old. In fact, cave and rock drawings suggest that skiing existed long before then, primarily as a means of hunting and travel. Norway is generally credited with developing the mode of transportation into a sport in the early 1700s. As interest in competition grew and as technological improvements in skis allowed for more control, alpine skiing was born. The disciplines of downhill and slalom became the ultimate tests of rapid descent and quick turns through some of nature's most challenging terrain. Today, alpine skiing events showcase stunning displays of balance, speed, and efficiency.

Several other winter competitions derived from practical functions. The biathlon, which combines cross-country skiing and shooting, evolved in Scandinavian countries for stalking prey, and later for military exercises. Bobsledding, which received its name from the bobbing motion riders make to increase the sled's progress, dates back to 1839, when the vehicles were used to carry wood.

Long periods of evolution, however, do not characterize all snow-oriented sports. Freestyle skiing, with its unconventional mogul jumps and pole flips, surfaced just 60 years ago and continues to expand its artistic limits. Another newcomer that emphasizes individuality and creativity—snowboarding—has garnered an avid following worldwide. These two outdoor activities may not share the history of the others, but, like all winter sports, enjoy enormous popularity.

This page (clockwise from top right): a snowboarder airborne on Buttermilk Mountain in Aspen, Colorado; children enjoying winter fun in the Rocky Mountains; a girl dogsledding; a World Cup Giant Slalom racer. Opposite page: a young figure skater in Aspen.

Madam
C. J.
Walker

January 28, 1998 • Indianapolis, Indiana

One of the most successful women entrepreneurs of the early 20th century, Madam C. J. Walker amassed a fortune with her international hair-care and cosmetic industry. But the prosperous businesswoman is perhaps best remembered for her astounding philanthropy and social activism. The U.S. Postal Service proudly honors Madam C. J. Walker's legacy with the 21st stamp in its Black Heritage series.

Born December 23, 1867, on a Delta, Louisiana cotton plantation, Walker labored as a laundress and cook before building her manufacturing empire. Not only did her hair-care business catapult her to personal wealth, but it also provided job opportunities for thousands of African-American women and men in the 1910s.

A champion of women's economic independence, she generously contributed to a variety of such causes and organizations. Though her resumé does not include any official awards of recognition during her lifetime, Walker was held in high esteem in the black community for her extraordinary philanthropy.

Walker's gestures of altruism were astonishing for an African-American woman of that era. Her gift of $1,000 to the black Indianapolis YMCA in 1912 was the single greatest donation from a black woman at the time. She donated $5,000 to the National Association for the Advancement of Colored People's Anti-Lynching Fund in 1919—the largest contribution the group had ever received before that year. Her contribution to the National Association of Colored Women's fund for the Frederick Douglass home in Washington, D.C., helped save the building from being sold. (It is currently a museum operated by the National Park Service and has been designated a National Historic Site).

Today, Madam C. J. Walker's spirit lives on across the country. Recently she was inducted into the National Women's Hall of Fame in Seneca Falls, New York, the National Cosmetology Hall of Fame in St. Louis, and the *Fortune*/Junior Achievement National Business Hall of Fame in Chicago.

This page (clockwise from top right): membership badge from a Walker convention; Walker driving in Indianapolis, Indiana, circa 1915; family members and employees at Madam C. J. Walker's estate in Irvington-on-Hudson, New York. Background: advertisement for Walker's hair products. Opposite page: entrepreneur and philanthropist, Madam C. J. Walker.

U.S. Battleship

Maine

Place
Stamp
Here

February 15, 1998 • Key West, Florida

On January 24, 1898, the U.S. Battleship *Maine* sailed from the peaceful waters of Key West, Florida, toward the embattled Spanish-ruled island of Cuba. Three weeks later, on a quiet evening in Havana Harbor, the vessel was destroyed by two powerful explosions. The final death figures totaled 266 officers and crew. The February 15 tragedy fueled the Spanish-American War and gave birth to the legendary slogan: "Remember the *Maine*."

Originally conceived as a British cruiser with sail, the ship was ultimately built in the United States and christened at the New York Navy Yard in Brooklyn on November 18, 1890. The purely American design made the *Maine* unique in the country's naval fleet. In 1896, the vessel headed south, responding to brewing unrest in Cuba. It was in the port of Key West that the crew of the battleship found a new home and formed a special bond with the locals. In 1897, the *Maine* provided a spectacular on-board Christmas light display for the Key West citizens.

But the relationship was short-lived. In January 1898, the *Maine* received orders from President McKinley to sail to Cuba on a "friendly visit." The three-week stay, however, came to an abrupt end with a marine mine blast, followed by a more powerful ammunition bunker explosion. In the aftermath of the horrible loss of life, a stunned nation's voice could be heard everywhere. Soon, "Remember the *Maine*" became America's rallying cry, appearing in newspaper headlines and on troop banners across the country.

This page (clockwise from top right): life ring and nautical Jack flag from the Maine; *the class ring, recovered in 1911, of the ship's junior engineering officer, Darwin Merritt; monument at the* Maine *Memorial Plot in Key West, Florida; burial of* Maine *victims at Arlington National Cemetery in Virginia. Background: explosion of the* Maine *in Havana Harbor, February 15, 1898. Opposite page: officers and crew of the U.S. Battleship* Maine.

In 1998, a series of commemorative events and a historic restoration of Key West's *Maine* Memorial Plot and Monument marked the occasion's centennial. A molded copper sailor stands upon the memorial, a hand raised above his eyes, as if straining to see his ship mates at Havana Harbor 90 miles away. The vessel's beloved home in Florida, and indeed the entire nation, shall always "remember the *Maine*."

Place
Stamps
Here

Flowering Trees

March 19, 1998 • New York, New York

From the coastal plains of the southeastern United States to the desert grasslands of the West, flowering trees not only span a broad geographical range but also exhibit an enormous diversity in appearance and use. The five trees represented on these stamps reflect this aesthetic and functional variety.

Primarily found from North Carolina to Texas, the Southern Magnolia has been labeled "the most splendid ornamental tree in the American forest." People admire it for the fragrant flowers and for the red seeds that hang by silken threads from its cone-shaped fruit. The Prairie Crab Apple, meanwhile, typically thrives in pastures of the Midwest and is distinguished by the dense hairiness it exhibits in the summer and by its smooth, pale green fruit. Heading farther west, one can discover the Pacific Dogwood, situated in the northwest plains and northern California mountains. This species, with its long, creamy white bracts and clustered red fruit, is most often cultivated for decorative value.

This page (clockwise from middle right): the Prairie Crab Apple, found in pastures and forest glades; greenish white flower of the Yellow Poplar; a Magnolia flower; Yellow Poplars in autumn. Opposite page: the Pacific Dogwood blooming in spring.

Visual appeal is just one aspect of these trees. For example, the Blue Paloverde, common in washes and desert grasslands in the Southwest, also serves several practical needs. Mountain sheep, deer, and smaller mammals feed on the tree's twigs and leaves, and the Native Americans of Arizona use the Paloverde's pods and seeds to make a thick soup. Indigenous to rich, moist soil, the Yellow Poplar—also called the tulip tree—can reach heights of 200 feet and was once used by early pioneers to build lightweight dugout canoes. The fruit of the Prairie Crab Apple is extracted to make tangy jams, while the fruit of the Pacific Dogwood—once prized for its medicinal value—today provides sustenance for many birds and animals.

Interest in flowering trees and other plant life is widespread. According to the American Association of Botanical Gardens and Arboreta, 50 million people visit public gardens and arboreta each year.

Alexander
Calder

March 25, 1998 · Washington, DC

During a career that spanned more than 50 years, Alexander Calder revolutionized the art world. Pioneer of the mobile and the similar yet stationary stabile, the sculptor created an array of dazzling public artwork.

Born in 1898 in Philadelphia, Calder was perhaps destined to be an artist: His father and grandfather were successful sculptors, and his mother was a painter. After studying mechanical engineering in college, Calder ventured to Paris in 1926. It was in the French capital that he found a second home and ultimately developed his unique approach to art. In his innovative performance of "Cirque Calder," the artist fabricated miniature wood-and-wire animals with movable parts. With the encouragement of several influential Parisian artists, the sculptor expanded the art form, using his engineering background to create a variety of kinetic abstract objects. His sculptures incorporated various types of motion—rotary, vertical, and oscillatory—reminiscent of planets in motion and often a reflection of the astronomical breakthroughs of the times. The term "mobile" was offered by artist Marcel Duchamp in 1932 to describe the genre, and it became Calder's enduring trademark.

> "A mobile is a piece of poetry that dances with the joy of life."
>
> *Alexander Calder*

The artist went on to fashion a variety of imaginative sculptures and even produced works with choreographed fountains. In the latter part of his career, he was commissioned to create monumental mobiles and stabiles in several countries, revitalizing the appearance of public art. Calder's sweeping metal-and-wire creations enhance cities around the globe.

This pane of U.S. Postal Service stamps, featuring five of the sculptor's works, coincides with the 100th anniversary of Calder's birth and pays tribute to his artistic legacy.

This page (clockwise from top right): Calder surrounded by his work; one of the artist's abstract sculptures; Calder posing with one of his sculptures in Saché, France. Background: silhouette of a Calder stabile. Opposite page: the artist preparing to paint a jetliner by practicing on a model.

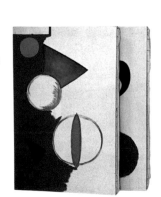

Works of Art © 1998 Estate of Alexander Calder/Artists Rights Society (ARS) New York

Cinco de Mayo

April 16, 1998 • San Antonio, Texas

Place
Stamp
Here

O riginally the date of a military victory more than a century ago, May 5—or "Cinco de Mayo"—is now one of the biggest holidays of the year for Americans of Mexican heritage. Celebrated in festive style, Cinco de Mayo today symbolizes a sense of cultural pride and identity.

The holiday recognizes the country's dramatic military stand against France on May 5, 1862, in Puebla, a town about 75 miles from Mexico City. Although France overwhelmed Mexico just a year later, the date is remembered for the small Mexican army's improbable victory over a superior French force— considered at the time the greatest military power in the world. The successful

This page (clockwise from top right): a Cinco de Mayo celebration in Austin, Texas; girl getting into the holiday spirit; children in traditional dress. Opposite page: young Hispanic girls in Cinco de Mayo costume.

campaign, led by General Ignacio Zaragoza, was so stunning that it kindled a newfound spirit of nationalism and resolve to defend the country's sovereignty. "*¡Viva el Cinco de Mayo!*" echoed across the proud nation. Once hopeless Mexicans came to the aid of their beleaguered country in the several years following the battle. By 1867, after the withdrawal of French troops to Europe, Mexico had finally regained its freedom.

Although Cinco de Mayo commemorates the fight to maintain Mexico's independence, the holiday has become a much bigger celebration in the United States. In fact, the first such festival took place in San Francisco in 1863, when a local businessman staged a Cinco de Mayo dance. By the mid-20th century, the date had evolved into a national fiesta, acquiring a fun festival atmosphere with parades, traditional foods, dancing, and the music of mariachi and other bands. Since then, Cinco de Mayo has gradually emerged as an opportunity for Mexican Americans to express pride in their heritage. No longer strictly a Mexican celebration, the holiday now promotes solidarity and fellowship among the entire Latin-American community.

Place
Stamps
Here

Sylvester
& Tweety

April 27, 1998 • New York, New York

When Sylvester and Tweety were teamed, their icon status was firmly cemented. Whether it was the clownish cat plotting hilarious schemes to obliterate his feathered foe, or the baby bird calmly and expertly turning the tables on his furry nemesis, very few duos have entertained and captured the hearts of so many. Sylvester and Tweety's joining performance in *Tweetie Pie* earned Warner Bros. its very first Academy Award for an animated short. The frenzied feline and blue-eyed bird became known as one of the most lovable cartoon couples ever.

The pair's antics invariably revolved around Sylvester's insatiable desire to devour his tiny yellow cohort. But Tweety was no easy target. The seemingly helpless, baby-talking bird had a sly and resourceful spirit lurking beneath those pristine feathers, and never failed to foil the cat's attacks. Tweety's wide-eyed "I tawt I taw a puddy tat!" has endured as a classic signature line.

But their appeal was no temporary fad. Over their illustrious careers, the clever and cuddly bird and bumbling but lovable cat garnered three Oscar nominations, winning the award twice. The acclaim and affection for Sylvester and Tweety live on today and have made them two of the most popular Looney Tunes characters ever.

The Sylvester and Tweety stamp is the second in a series featuring popular Looney Tunes characters from Warner Bros. In 1997, a stamp honoring that "wascally wabbit," Bugs Bunny, was issued.

This page (counterclockwise from top left): the watchful canary sitting on a swing in Tweet Dreams; *Sylvester licking his chops in* Tweety's S.O.S.; *the famished feline duped again in* Bad Ol' Putty Tat. *Background: the flustered feline. Opposite page: Sylvester with his feathered foe in sight in* Bad Ol' Putty Tat.

Place
Stamp
Here

Wisconsin Statehood

May 29, 1998 · Madison, Wisconsin

The area now known as Wisconsin was first inhabited by Native Americans more than 10,000 years ago. Of the earliest such groups, the Woodland Indians left behind the most evidence of their way of life. One such vestige is the 12,000 effigy mounds scattered throughout the state, of which more than 200 still remain in and around the state capital of Madison.

White settlement, however, marked the end of Native American control in the area. Explored by the French in the 17th century, ethnic groups from all over Europe migrated to the state in large numbers starting in the mid-19th century. The largest such group were the Germans, who began arriving in the 1840s to escape political and religious persecution. In fact, Wisconsin has the highest German representation in the United States.

Lead mining became an important industry in the state in the early 19th century. Workers often sought shelter in makeshift hillside burrows, and were thus dubbed "badgers." The animal epithet gradually gained acceptance as an appropriate metaphor for the hardworking spirit of early settlers, hence giving birth to Wisconsin's eventual nickname, the "Badger State." In 1848, Wisconsin entered the Union, becoming the nation's 30th state.

By the end of the 19th century, the state emerged as a dairy leader. Long known as "America's Dairyland," today Wisconsin ranks at or near the top in dairy and other agricultural production.

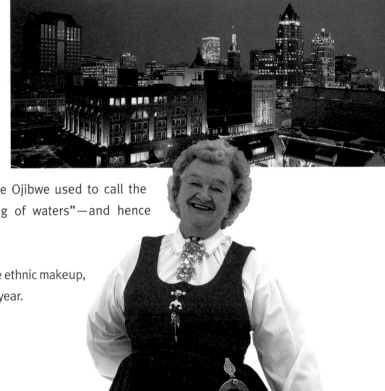

This page (clockwise from top right): autumn at a farm in Kewaunee County, Wisconsin; Milwaukee skyline at night; Wisconsin woman in Norwegian dress; feathers at a traditional tribal powwow in Hayward. Background: Wisconsin coat of arms. Opposite page: The Chippewa River flowing through the Chequamegon National Forest.

Lying amid the Upper Great Lakes, Wisconsin offers a splendid panorama of rolling hills, valleys, lakes, and shoreline—an ideal environment for camping and fishing, two of the state's most popular recreations. The beautiful Wisconsin River, which winds over 400 miles, is actually not named after the state, but vice versa: The Ojibwe used to call the flow "Wees-konsan"—meaning "gathering of waters"—and hence the state name.

Known for both its natural beauty and diverse ethnic makeup, Wisconsin celebrates its 150th birthday this year.

Place
Stamp
Here

Trans-

June 18, 1998 • Anaheim, California

Following the Louisiana Purchase and the journeys of Lewis and Clark, America embarked on a mission to explore and uncover the American West. It was under this climate of trailblazing spirit and courage that the Trans-Mississippi and International Exposition was born.

Held in Omaha, Nebraska, in 1898, the five-month exposition was staged to promote progress and development in the area west of the Mississippi River. To mark the affair, the U.S. Post Office Department planned to issue a series of bi-color commemorative stamps—only the second such series ever released—depicting the triumph and tragedy of early Western settlers. While the intent was admirable, the timing could not have been worse. In February of that year, the U.S.S. *Maine* was destroyed in Havana Harbor, thrusting the nation into battle with Spain. Burdened with war-induced manpower and monetary restrictions, the collection had to be altered severely. The two-color printing plan was abruptly canceled, and some of the originally promised illustrations were never used.

Amid the war-driven revisions, the series nonetheless flourished as one of the most sought-after collections ever. Many of the unsold stamps were recalled and destroyed within a year, magnifying the collection's significance and mystique. The designs themselves are admired for their delicately wrought, powerful images. "Western Cattle in Storm," featured here, is regarded by many to be the most visually spectacular postage stamp ever. For nearly a century, however, the altered monochrome series left collectors frustrated, wondering what could have been.

One hundred years later, these questions are answered at last. In recognition of the Trans-Mississippi Exposition's centennial anniversary, the U.S. Postal Service is proud to reissue the collection in its originally planned two-color print. The full nine-stamp series is finally here—the way it was intended.

This page (clockwise from top right): Emanuel Leutze's Westward the Course of Empire Takes Its Way; *Horticultural Building at the Trans-Mississippi and International Exposition, Omaha, Nebraska, 1898; Government Building at the Exposition. Background: map of the Exposition grounds. Opposite page: Jackson Pollock's* Going West, *1934-35.*

Mississippi
Reissue of 1898

Place
Stamp
Here

Berlin Airlift

June 26, 1998 · Berlin, Germany

Conflicts of willpower and resolve characterized much of the Cold War era, and one of the first major tests was the Berlin Airlift. Overcoming ideological and logistical obstacles, the 1948-49 Allied mission was an extremely significant and impressive peacetime supply effort in an early standoff with the Soviet Union.

Following World War II, Germany was occupied by the four major Allies from the war in Europe—the United States, Britain, France, and the Soviet Union. Germany's capital, Berlin, had been split into four sectors as well, but lay deep inside the Russian zone. After a currency dispute in the summer of 1948, the Soviets blocked land and water access to the city, leaving only narrow air corridors for Allied access. The Soviet goal was not so much to starve the people of Berlin as it was to make them depend on Soviet resources. Rather than resorting to armed conflict or conceding altogether, Allied forces united to airlift food and fuel to the blockaded city. The mission—also known as Operation Vittles—proved a huge success. The airlifted goods supplied Berliners for more than a year, ultimately forcing the blockade's removal.

The logistics of the operation were difficult, to say the least. Yet the Allied effort was remarkably persistent—and consistent—in meeting the challenge. Planes commonly arrived in Berlin at three-minute intervals around the clock. Every single day of the airlift, at least one transport delivered supplies—regardless of weather, maintenance difficulties, or threatening maneuvers by Soviet aircraft. During the operation, the airlift delivered a total of nearly 2.5 million tons of goods. Led by Maj. Gen. William H. Tunner, the airlift spanned the 11 tense months of the blockade and continued for four more as surface transportation was restored. Said Tunner of the mission's objectives: "The Berlin Airlift was definitely capable of either breaking the blockade, or of maintaining life in Berlin while negotiations were going on." Indeed, in May of 1949, the Soviets lifted the blockade.

This page (clockwise from top right): Berliners unloading food from a plane; fresh milk being packed aboard aircraft at Rhein-Main Air Base; appreciative Berlin residents waving to an approaching airlift plane. Background: occupation zones in Germany, 1944-1945. Opposite page: airlift planes flying over Berlin with food and coal.

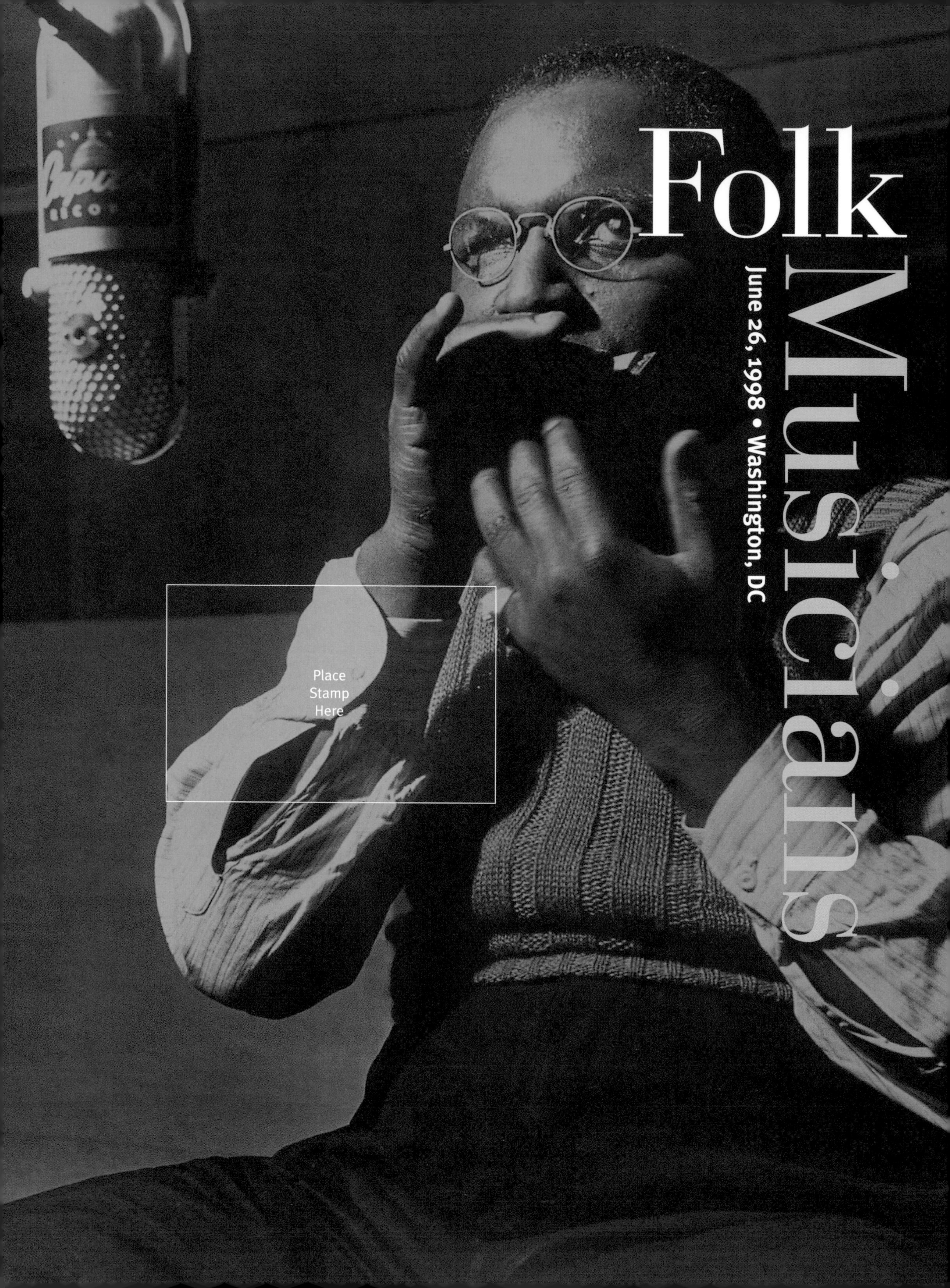

Folk Musicians

June 26, 1998 • Washington, DC

Place
Stamp
Here

Few performers captured the essence of the folk revival better than Huddie Ledbetter, Woody Guthrie, Sonny Terry, and Josh White. The Legends of American Music series proudly salutes these four musicians for their unforgettable talents.

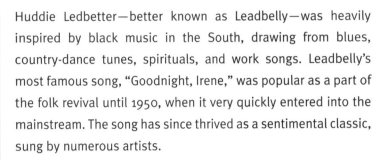

Huddie Ledbetter—better known as Leadbelly—was heavily inspired by black music in the South, drawing from blues, country-dance tunes, spirituals, and work songs. Leadbelly's most famous song, "Goodnight, Irene," was popular as a part of the folk revival until 1950, when it very quickly entered into the mainstream. The song has since thrived as a sentimental classic, sung by numerous artists.

"This Land Is Your Land" has become an unofficial national anthem, but its hopeful, unifying message is atypical of its author, Woody Guthrie—the consummate folk singer. Of the roughly 1,000 songs written by Guthrie, this one surfaced as a beacon of promise during the lean years of the Great Depression. Writing the words, Guthrie invoked his travels across the United States, particularly through the far West. The song has taken on a life of its own, transcending political and social divisions and becoming emblematic of the ideal America.

This page (clockwise from top right): Woody Guthrie with his guitar; harmonica virtuoso Sonny Terry; Josh White, circa 1945; Leadbelly performing. Opposite page: Sonny Terry playing harmonica.

Sonny Terry, who was blind virtually all of his life, is remembered not only for his instrumental mastery, but also for his animated and inspired showmanship. "The Fox Chase" perhaps best illustrates this enthusiasm, with his energetic harmonica playing and distinctive yelping and whooping. Terry's amazing musical ability earned the admiration of both fans and fellow blues and folk musicians.

Renowned for his exceptional guitar playing, Josh White played primarily in the southeastern blues tradition, drawing from both sacred and secular black music. Actively performing for more than 40 years, he fostered a deep sense of social protest during much of his career. "Free and Equal Blues" reflected these themes, emerging as one of White's most powerful ballads.

Place
Stamp
Here

Gospel
Singers

July 15, 1998 • New Orleans, Louisiana

The voices of four celebrated female singers—Mahalia Jackson, Roberta Martin, Sister Rosetta Tharpe, and Clara Ward—will forever resonate in the classic gospel tradition. These popular performers are honored by the Legends of American Music stamp series for their exceptional talents.

"When you sing gospel, you have a feeling there is a cure for what's wrong."

Mahalia Jackson

Born in New Orleans, Mahalia Jackson moved as a teenager to Chicago in 1927. It was there that she began to sing professionally. Jackson's "Move On Up a Little Higher" in 1947 sold more than three million copies and quickly earned her the title, "Gospel Queen." Although she was not the first gospel singer, she did garner international acclaim and is largely credited with exposing people of all races to the music.

Like Jackson, Roberta Martin also moved from the South to Chicago as an adolescent. Studying piano as a young child, she intended to become a concert pianist someday. In 1933, she began playing with five other performers, and the group became known as the Roberta Martin Singers. Publishing music through her own record company, Martin enjoyed a career marked by sophisticated gospel melodies and exotic harmonies.

At the age of ten, Clara Ward was already the accompanist for the Ward Trio, a family group consisting of her mother and sister. The group came to public attention in 1943, touring throughout the Southeast, and eventually becoming known as the Ward Singers. Ward's powerful contralto voice and stunning talent as an arranger, composer, and pianist established her as one of the most versatile gospel singers ever.

This page (clockwise from top right): cover of Roberta Martin sheet music; Clara Ward singing; Sister Rosetta Tharpe, circa 1944. Background: music and words for "So High, So Low" by Sister Rosetta. Opposite page: the "Gospel Queen," Mahalia Jackson.

Sister Rosetta Tharpe developed a reputation as a singer-evangelist in Chicago before moving to New York. There she quickly gained fame for her electrifying live performances. In 1938, she performed with both Cab Calloway and Benny Goodman. Playing in theaters and churches, Sister Rosetta emerged as a gospel star remembered for her bright voice and vivid guitar playing.

I'VE GOT TO CROSS OVER TO SEE MY LORD

ARRANGED by Evelyn ROBERTA MARTIN

PRICE 20 CENTS

PUBLISHED BY
THE MARTIN STUDIO OF GOSPEL MUSIC
69½ EAST 43RD ST., CHICAGO 15, ILL.

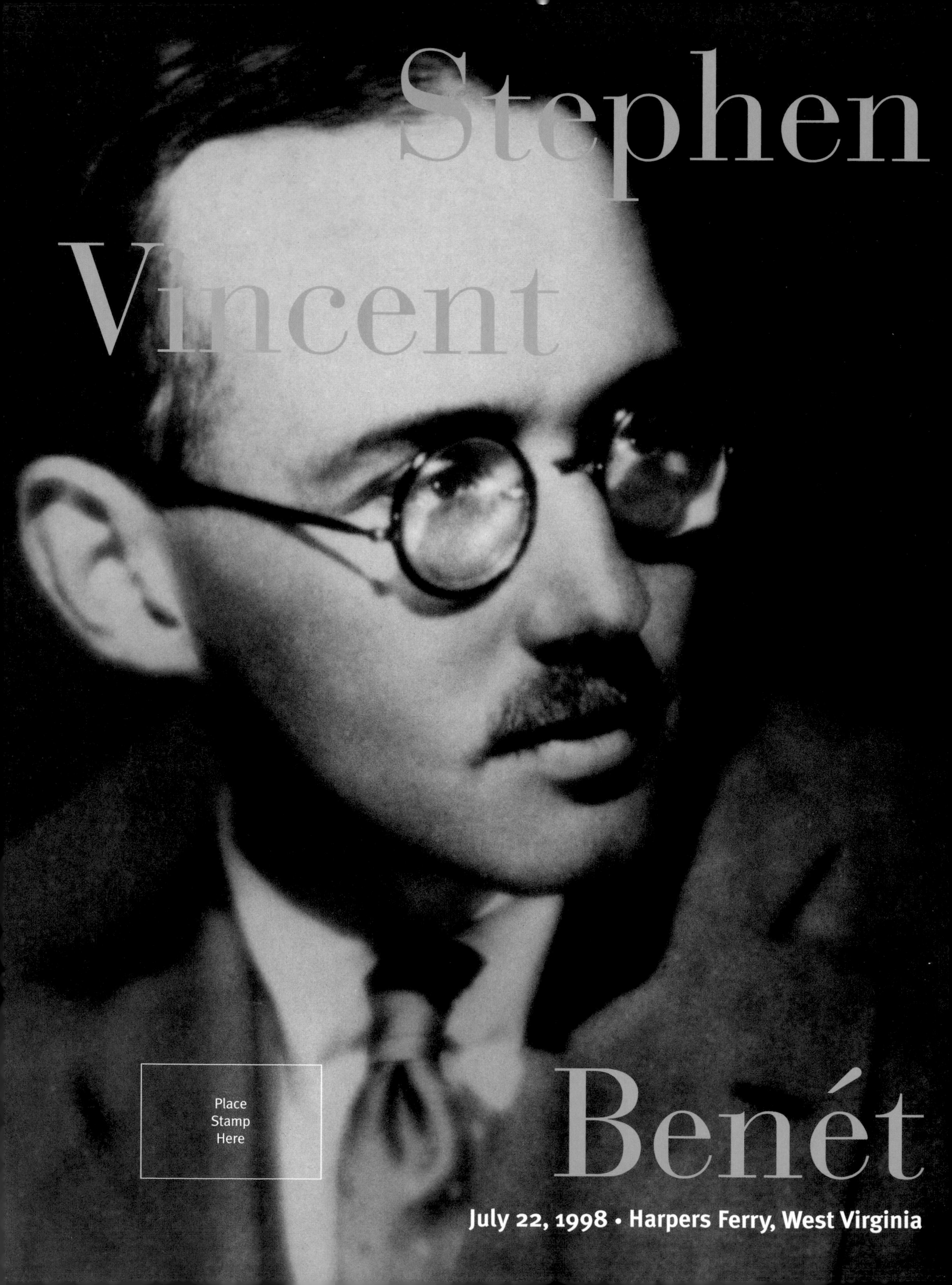

Stephen

Vincent

Benét

July 22, 1998 · Harpers Ferry, West Virginia

With a legacy marked by both popular and critical acclaim, Stephen Vincent Benét remains one of the most celebrated writers in American history. One hundred years after his birth, his award-winning works are remembered for their distinctly American themes and brilliant combination of myth and history.

Stephen Vincent Benét was born on July 22, 1898, in Bethlehem, Pennsylvania. The son of a career military officer, he grew up with a keen interest in American military history and literature as a whole. He began his writing career at Yale University, serving as chairman of the editorial board of the school's literary magazine and publishing his first book of poetry, *Five Men and Pompey*. The aspiring writer was rejected for military service because of poor eyesight, and worked briefly at the State Department before returning to Yale to graduate in 1919.

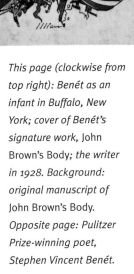

In 1926, Benét went to Paris on a Guggenheim Fellowship. It was there that he wrote perhaps his most famous work, *John Brown's Body*, an epic poem chronicling Civil War events from the raid on Harper's Ferry to General Lee's surrender at Appomatox. The narrative epitomized Benét's skillful blend of fact with poetic power. The book won him his first Pulitzer Prize in 1929 and is regarded by many as the quintessential American war poem. Although he was criticized by some for his loosely structured, sentimental style, Benét was widely acclaimed for his grasp of history and powerful depictions of American legends.

This page (clockwise from top right): Benét as an infant in Buffalo, New York; cover of Benét's signature work, John Brown's Body; *the writer in 1928. Background: original manuscript of* John Brown's Body. *Opposite page: Pulitzer Prize-winning poet, Stephen Vincent Benét.*

The author wrote not only novels and poems, but also plays, historical essays, and short stories—his most well-known being "The Devil and Daniel Webster," which captured the O. Henry Memorial Prize in 1936. Benét worked for the Office of War Information during World War II until his death in 1943.

Place
Stamp
Here

Tropical Birds

July 29, 1998 • Puerto Rico

Today, more than 70 million North Americans take to the outdoors in the hopes of spying their favorite feathered fauna. In fact, half of the people in this country consider themselves "active birders," according to the American Birding Association. This stamp block depicts four colorful birds found throughout America's tropical islands.

The Antillean Euphonia can be found in Puerto Rico, as well as in Hispaniola and the Lesser Antilles. It generally favors thick mountain forests, such as Puerto Rico's Luquillo Mountains. A sky-blue crown and nape distinguish the bird from similar species, and explain one of its former names—Blue-hooded Euphonia. Like most in the tanager family, this bird feeds almost exclusively on fruits.

Indigenous to the northern coast of Puerto Rico and parts of the Virgin Islands, the Green-throated Carib is a hummingbird capable of beating its wings nearly 50 times per second. The name "Carib" derives from the Carib Indians who were exterminated in Puerto Rico and the Virgin Islands by European conquerors. The bird, which has a sapphire-blue mark on its front, uses its curved and pointed bill to probe flowers for insects and its long, tubular tongue to suck nectar.

Distinguished by its forward-directed bushy crest that transfers pollen between flowers, the Crested Honeycreeper generally likes to feed on nectar. An endangered species that used to be found on Molokai in the Hawaiian Islands, the bird today inhabits only the upper rain forests of Maui. Like other Hawaiian birds, the species is capable of producing humanlike whistles, wheezy notes, and gutteral buzzes.

The Cardinal Honeyeater is found in Samoa and has close relatives in Micronesia (including Guam) and other Pacific islands. Males feature a black tail, belly, and wings with a scarlet breast; females, however, are grayish olive with scarlet rumps. An acrobatic bird, it is common in towns and villages, often feeding on flowers around homes.

Alfred

August 3, 1998 • Los Angeles, California

Place
Stamp
Here

Hitchcock

Perhaps no other filmmaker in history was as adept at feeding the public's appetite for "thrills and chills" as Alfred Joseph Hitchcock. During a career that spanned over half a century, the "Master of Suspense" captivated audiences with powerful films built on mounting anxiety, haunting realism, and even surprising humor. The U.S. Postal Service proudly recognizes Hitchcock as part of its Legends of Hollywood series.

Born in 1899 in London, Hitchcock debuted behind the camera in 1923. It was his direction of *The Pleasure Garden* two years later, however, that launched his brilliant career and eventually sent him to Hollywood. There he stayed until his death in 1980, directing scores of psychological thrillers and producing hundreds of harrowing episodes for his very own *Alfred Hitchcock Presents*. It was on this television series that his self-caricature profile became known to millions, and it endures as the Hitchcock trademark.

The director brought a distinct visual style to American cinema. Whether it was the curious lighting of a possibly fatal glass of milk in 1941's *Suspicion* or the dizzying close-up montages in 1958's *Vertigo*, Hitchcock was an expert manipulator. He once remarked on his filmmaking philosophy, "There is no terror in the bang, only in the anticipation of it." Hitchcock was, however, interested in more than shock value. His films have stood out for their delicate balance of terror and humor—ordinary and absurd. Behind many blood-chilling scenes lay undercurrents of comic relief or bizarre irony.

This witty edge was a reflection of Hitchcock himself. Famous for his dry, outrageous comments, the rotund director made cameo appearances in nearly all of his own films, often with a funny twist. In perhaps his most memorable picture, the shower-slasher *Psycho*, his portly silhouette appears through the window—wearing a cowboy hat. Reflecting on his directing goals, Hitchcock once summarized with characteristic incision, "Always make the audience suffer as much as possible."

Alfred Hitchcock ™ & © The Alfred Hitchcock Trust
Alfred Hitchcock Presents © Universal Studios

*T*he Legends of Hollywood series began with a stamp honoring American beauty and talent Marilyn Monroe, and continued with the sexy rebel James Dean, and the cool, self-confident Humphrey Bogart. The series now features the "Master of Suspense," Alfred Hitchcock.

Hitchcock made numerous cameos in his own films. A few of his appearances include: being bothered by a boy while reading in the subway in 1929's Blackmail; *leaving a train with a cello case in 1947's* The Paradine Case; *and leaving a pet shop with two white terriers in 1963's* The Birds.

Place
Stamp
Here

Organ
&Tissue
Donation

August 5, 1998 • Columbus, Ohio

I n 1968, Dr. Norman Shumway of Stanford University Hospital performed the first successful heart transplant. This year marks the 30th anniversary of that miraculous achievement and reminds us all of the importance of giving the gift of life. Today, thousands of lives are saved each year through organ and tissue donations, but the need for transplants still far outpaces the supply.

More than 60,000 Americans are awaiting lifesaving organ transplants, and hundreds of thousands more could benefit from tissue transplants. Despite technical and pharmaceutical advances in transplantation, ten people die each day for lack of donated organs. The Coalition on Donation was formed to undertake the first major national public education program to promote organ and issue donation. A partnership with the Federal Government resulted in donation information being sent to 70 million Americans in their 1996 income tax refunds. "For those Americans who need transplants, it's a race against time," said Senator Bill Frist of Tennessee, who is also a transplant surgeon. "By signing a card and talking to their families about that decision, more and more Americans can provide a chance for more winners in this race." All public education efforts are centered around the phrase, *Organ and Tissue Donation: Share your life. Share your decision*. This message emphasizes the importance of making the decision and then communicating with family members so they can carry out the plan.

The science of transplantation has progressed steadily since its origins in the 18th century. By 1970, several human organs had been transplanted successfully, and recent scientific breakthroughs in tissue typing have provided even more encouragement. All of this medical progress, however, cannot overcome the need for more organ and tissue donations.

For a brochure about organ and tissue donation and how to discuss this important decision with your family, call 1-800-355-SHARE (7427). *Organ and Tissue Donation: Share your life. Share your decision.*

This page (clockwise from top right): Dr. Joseph E. Murray, credited with the first successful kidney transplant in 1954; Dr. Norman Shumway, after completing the first successful heart transplant; organ donor card. Opposite page: three surgeons performing a kidney transplant in Denver, Colorado.

My Commitment To Share Life
Uniform Donor Card

I, _____ have spoken to my family about organ and tissue, donation. The following people have witnessed my commitment to be a donor. I wish to donate: ☐ any organs and tissues ☐ only the following organs and tissues:_____

Donor Signature_____ Date_____
Witness_____ Date_____
Witness_____ Date_____

Bright

August 20, 1998 • City, State TBD

Place
Stamp
Here

Eyes

Americans love their pets, and the more playful and cuddly, the better. This stamp collection—featuring charming images of the ever popular dog and cat, as well as the goldfish, parakeet, and hamster—is for pet owners and animal lovers of all ages.

The popularity of these animals is remarkable. The number of pet-owning households has reached close to 60 million, representing more than half of American residences. There are more than 10,000 retail pet stores across the country, accounting for several billion dollars of annual sales.

Dogs have been called "man's best friend," and, indeed, of all domesticated animals, they have the longest history of friendship with humans. Providing protection and hunting skills for hundreds of years, dogs have always been trusted aids. But more than anything, canines are cherished for their companionship and loyalty. Owners appreciate their four-legged comrades for their variety of sizes, colors, shapes, and even personalities. Although more than a hundred breeds are recognized in the United States, the most popular dogs include the labrador retriever, rottweiler, German shepherd, golden retriever, beagle, and poodle.

Millions of Americans love charming and playful animals, including (clockwise from top right): cuddly dogs; pint-size parakeets; frisky hamsters; and goldfish. Opposite page: bright-eyed cat and dog lounging in chair.

Cats also receive much of our love and attention. In fact, there are currently more felines gracing American homes than dogs. Much like their canine counterparts, cats offer endless comfort and affection, with pint-size appeal and sly charm. From poofy Persians to shorthaired Siamese, felines of all kinds are loved by millions.

Birds, small animals, and fish have also captured the hearts of Americans. Our feathered, furry, and freshwater friends can be found in more than 20 million households. Although they are unlikely to enjoy the lifespan of dogs and cats, pets such as parakeets, hamsters, and goldfish provide the same wide-eyed innocence and lovable companionship.

Klondike
Gold Rush

August 21, 1998 • Nome, Alaska

Place
Stamp
Here

George Washington Carmack. Tagish Charlie. Skookum Jim. They may not be household names, but the trio will forever be legends of the Klondike Gold Rush. In 1896, these men discovered gold in the Yukon's Rabbit Creek, fueling a massive influx of hopeful prospectors to the Klondike River region. The pilgrimage through Alaska and the Canadian West, however, proved tortuous and painful, with most explorers never finding their fortune.

This page (clockwise from top right): the steamship Rosalie leaving for the Klondike, circa 1900; a miner digging for gold in the Klondike; prospectors on a lake in the Yukon Territory; the Klondike Trading Company's store, circa 1900. Opposite page: Klondikers trudging through the Chilkoot Pass in Alaska, circa 1898.

As soon as word spread of the windfall at Rabbit Creek—later named Bonanza Creek—the rush was on. Dreaming of striking it rich, people left their homes and headed to Canada. The once impoverished Pacific Northwest flourished on the trade and travel of gold diggers. Soon, more than 100,000 voyagers had stampeded toward the Klondike. But the reality was harsh. Crossing treacherous Alaskan mountain passes and swamps, travelers, often with inadequate supplies, suffered through hardships such as subzero temperatures and vicious mosquitoes. Dozens of would-be miners were killed by an avalanche at the infamous Chilkoot Pass.

Those who persevered, however, arrived joyfully in towns like Dawson, where a thriving community was born. Klondikers reveled in their vibrant new home, which teemed with gold mines, saloons, and a raucous nightlife. Gambling, dance halls, and whiskey were the order of the day. The festive atmosphere, however, quickly dissolved after the rush peaked in 1898. The best claims had been staked, and most settlers trudged home empty-handed. In fact, of the few thousand who did find gold, only a handful actually became wealthy, and most of them squandered away their fortunes.

Today, 100 years after the pinnacle of the Klondike Gold Rush, the trek's romantic image and brutal truths live on. Perhaps Robert Service's poem, "The Spell of the Yukon," best captures the iron-willed spirit and bleak reality of the journey: "I wanted the gold, and I sought it, I scrabbled and mucked like a slave. Was it famine or scurvy—I fought it; I hurled my youth into a grave."

Four
Centuries of

August 27, 1998 • Santa Clara, California

Place
Stamp
Here

American Art

From the monochrome portraits of the 17th century to the sweeping conceptual paintings of today, American art has evolved dramatically. Many of the visual themes, however, have remained remarkably similar. The U.S. Postal Service's Classic Collection of 20 masterpieces reflects both the variety in styles and the consistency in subjects of American art over the past four centuries.

The artists featured were born in many parts of this country, and a few were born abroad. Some were professionally trained, while others—such as Joshua Johnson and Ammi Phillips—were self-taught. Johnson was the first African American to become a professional painter. He was probably born a slave, but by the time he began painting portraits in the 1790s, he was a free man.

Despite the diversity of the artists, their paintings depict recurring topics characteristic of the American tradition. One such focus is the spirit of expansionism and adventure. George Caleb Bingham's *Boatmen on the Missouri,* and Winslow Homer's *The Fog Warning,* for instance, portray solid, determined individuals exploring and conquering natural frontiers. Indeed, veneration for the variety of landscapes across the continent permeates American art, especially 19th-century expressions. Thomas Moran's *Cliffs of Green River* and Frederic Edwin Church's *Niagara* reveal grand natural panoramas in dramatic detail.

Down-to-earth realism is another theme common to American art, particularly beginning in the late 19th century. Mary Cassatt's *Breakfast in Bed* radiates the warm tenderness of a woman and child, while Grant Wood's *American Gothic* is a prime example of Regionalism, reflecting a spirit of self-reliance during the lean years of the Great Depression. *Nighthawks* by Edward Hopper demonstrates similar realism with stark lighting and expressionless faces, and suggests urban alienation.

By the middle of the 20th century, a new artistic direction had developed in America—Abstract Expressionism. The style stresses nonrepresentational images. Works such as Franz Kline's *Mahoning* and Mark Rothko's *No. 12* incorporate respectively colliding strokes and zones of color that invite more subjective interpretation.

This page (clockwise from top right): Mary Cassatt's Sara in a Green Bonnet, *circa 1901; Thomas Moran's* The Grand Canyon of the Yellowstone; *Winslow Homer in Prout's Neck, Maine, posing at his easel with* The Gulf Stream, *detail. Opposite page: Winslow Homer's* The Reaper.

Ballet

September 16, 1998 · New York, New York

F rom Parisian theaters to small-town dance studios, the elegance and beauty of ballet is enjoyed around the globe. This dramatic stamp honors students and professionals alike who are passionate about the world of dance.

Ballet has evolved considerably over several centuries. Originating in Italy, the style of dance has spread across the globe and can no longer be easily defined. Generally a ballet tells a story, but sometimes, particularly in modern ballet, there is no plot. Beautiful music usually accompanies the dancing; on occasion, however, ballets may not contain any music, and may even feature singing or speeches by the characters. In a more general sense, ballet can be defined as the root of all Western theatrical dance. Indeed, most people aspiring to become professional dancers are encouraged to begin with ballet.

The study of the dance form in the United States began rather inauspiciously. The School of American Ballet opened in 1934 during the Great Depression to an American population that lacked classical dance traditions. But with the finances and vision of its founders, Lincoln Kirstein and George Balanchine, the school flourished, spawning the equally prosperous New York City Ballet in 1948.

Today, students of all ages study ballet. The typical lesson consists mainly of stretching, position, balance, and step sequences. The dance form exhibits a variety of peculiar techniques, most notably skipping on one's toes. The method, called "on pointe," creates the weightless, elegant appearance so often associated with the performance. One of the other distinguishing elements of ballet is that dancers typically stand with their hips and legs turned out—primarily for greater flexibility—with shoes that have paper-thin soles and no heels. Such unique positions and techniques, while physically demanding, combine to create the ethereal beauty special to ballet.

This page (clockwise from top right): dance students warming up for class; performance of one of the most well-known ballets, The Nutcracker; *tools of the trade: a pair of ballet shoes. Background: Elie Nadelman's* Dancer, *circa 1918-1919, in cherry-wood. Opposite page:* The Green Dancer (Dancers on the Stage), *in pastel and gouache, by Edgar Degas.*

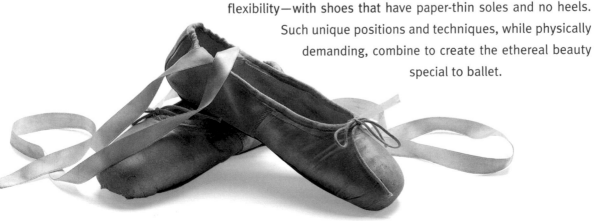

Spacery

Discovery

October 1, 1998
Kennedy Space Center, Florida

Place
Stamp
Here

Who or what lies beyond our planet remains one of life's greatest mysteries. But that hasn't stopped us earthlings from dreaming up a vast array of fantasy worlds. These spectacular stamps capture the marvelous and exciting prospects of space discovery.

Envisioning faraway galaxies has challenged the minds and fired the imaginations of adults and youths alike. From colonizing remote planets to building lunar bases to zooming through the stars, we have pictured a variety of potential expeditions. These visions reflect our never ending optimism and curiosity about exploring, and even inhabiting, space. But as much as flights of fancy spark our creative spirit, the wonder of nature itself inspires equal awe. Astronomical discoveries and increasing knowledge of our solar system have prodded us to base speculation on sound scientific theories. In fact, space fantasy has generally preceded actual 20th century developments. Early science fiction stories described man someday penetrating our atmosphere and landing on the moon. Soon, that dream was realized. Still others conceptualized one day making contact with Mars. Sure enough, we have successfully landed a rover on the Red Planet.

This page (clockwise from top right): NASA's International Cometary Explorer; a spiral galaxy; robot from sci-fi movie Gog; an astronaut drifting above the Earth's atmosphere. Background: various planetary bodies. Opposite page: futuristic space scene by artist Attila Hejja.

The notion of space travel has truly captivated us. Most sci-fi stories depict dramatic spacecraft darting through the heavens at speeds faster than light. Some suggest time travel, and a few have even conjectured that a space ship, entering a black hole, can emerge in another universe. Although issues of propulsion and life support are generally exaggerated, actual scientific facts are incorporated into our visions of galactic flight.

One interesting tendency of space fantasy is to show humans solving age-old conflicts in the context of a distant cosmos. This idealism is perhaps reflective of what we hope other worlds can represent. Indeed, today we continue to be inspired by the wonderful possibilities that lay ahead in outer space.

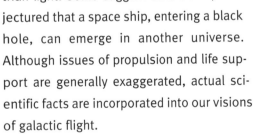

53

Giving & Sharing: Philanthropy

October 7, 1998 · Atlanta, Georgia

Place Stamp Here

American Red Cross

Ready For A New Century!

Whether it's hammering nails to build a house or donating money to a charity, philanthropy has always been an integral part of America. This stamp, depicting the giving-and-sharing relationship of a bee and flower, honors all those who generously contribute to their favorite causes.

Americans give to a variety of charities, with considerable donations going to health and relief groups. Disease-related agencies such as the American Heart Association and the American Cancer Society have garnered significant support. These groups often receive contributions from grateful patients and families who have benefitted from them. Some donors are simply concerned that they may one day need the services of such a health-oriented association. For relief groups, support is often fueled by natural disasters. The American Red Cross, for example, provides daily briefings to news services during disasters, thus capturing the attention and financial assistance of the public in order to help those in need.

Social, cultural, and educational organizations have widespread backing as well. The National Association for the Advancement of Colored People, for example, fights for the rights of minority groups everywhere and has branches in all 50 states. Many such causes receive substantial support from concerned citizens.

Some philanthropists, however, prefer a more proactive approach. Numerous volunteer organizations offer programs that provide hands-on assistance to the needy. From dishing out food at soup kitchens to counseling troubled youths, many Americans offer their time, rather than their money.

One example of such goodwill is building homes. Millions in this country are unable to afford adequate shelter for themselves and their families. By donating a few days of manual labor, volunteers have answered the call for many languishing in poverty. One such participant, Jimmy Carter, led a program that provided homes for some four dozen families in 1997. Summed up the former President: "We have become small players in an exciting global effort to alleviate the curse of homelessness."

October 15, 1998 • Washington, DC

Madonna and

The exquisite *Madonna and Child* relief featured on this stamp is the product of a Florentine terracotta workshop. Although several recognized artists of the era have been suggested as the creator of the circa 1425 piece, scholars continue to debate the identity of the exceptionally talented master who made it.

Florentine painters achieved great innovations from the 13th to the 16th century. Outstanding practitioners in this field included Giotto, Masaccio, Botticelli, Leonardo, and Michelangelo. Florentine sculptors, like the maker of this Madonna, proved no less brilliant. Two of the greatest, Ghiberti and Donatello, have sometimes been proposed as its sculptor.

This half-length relief is among the most striking and best preserved examples of polychromed and gilded terracotta reliefs, which were in demand for display both in homes and churches. Its combination of strong modeling and graceful conception of the figures places it among the finest examples of its kind.

The relief marks a milestone, not only for its superior craftsmanship, but also for its sympathetic depiction of the subjects. The energetic child, twisting and reaching for his mother's veil, introduces a playful and human quality to the sacred image. The cascading ornamental folds of Mary's garments reflect the courtly style of the early 15th century in Europe. But the child, freed of his princely robes and heavy wrappings of earlier periods, demonstrates the new Renaissance appreciation for the human body.

Though its artist remains shrouded in mystery, all can appreciate the *Madonna and Child*'s elegant beauty, phenomenal preservation, and human realism. The relief is on display at the National Gallery of Art in Washington, D.C.

This page (counterclockwise from top left): Madonna and Child mosaic from the 12th century; Luca della Robbia's Madonna of the Apple, from the National Museum of the Bargello in Florence, Italy; Virgin of Jeanne d'Evreux, circa 1330. Background: the Duomo, Milan, Italy. Opposite page: Andy Warhol's Untitled (Madonna and Child), gold leaf, stamped collage, ink and dye on paper.

Child

Place
Stamps
Here

Holiday
Wreaths

October 15, 1998 • Christmas, Michigan

Enduring symbols of the holiday season, wreaths can reflect both a spirit of fellowship and a distinct regional flavor. The U.S. Postal Service pays tribute to these four holiday wreaths—designed by prominent American floral stylists—for their aesthetic and geographic diversity.

The Fresh Green Wreath is a conspicuous reminder of the festive time of year with its beautiful cluster of pinecones and red ribbon. This garland, designed in the heart of the Pacific Northwest, has a noble fir base, illuminated by incense cedar and holly leaves.

Emblazoned with the vibrant colors of the Southwest, the Chili Wreath is marked by its air-dried chilies and dashes of corn husk. Designed in Baja, California, it sports distinctive Indian corn "flowers" that immediately suggest its region.

On the opposite coast, the Williamsburg Wreath features groupings of pomegranates, pinecones, tallow berries, and nut varieties. This colonial garland has touches of gold, intensified by a lemon leaf and preserved cedar base.

This page (clockwise from top right): a traditional holiday spray from Williamsburg, Virginia; plaza decorated with red chili wreaths in Velarde, New Mexico; a wreath in Santa Fe, New Mexico; a floral wreath on the door welcoming visitors. Opposite page: horns and fruit adorning a holiday wreath.

Bright summer hues are featured in the Tropical Wreath. Common to the Southeast and Hawaii, this holiday garland is noted for its brilliant tulip anthuriums that adorn the green hibiscus leaf base. Three orchid varieties—purple vandas, pink phalaenopsis, and yellow miniature cattleyas—enhance the wreath's tropical style.

The history of wreaths dates back to approximately 1000 B.C. when Greeks used them for a variety of purposes. Primarily used to attract good spirits and ward off evil ones, the decorations were typically hung on house doors and windows. Some garlands were purchased as emblems of wisdom, while others were cherished for their supposed healing powers. Indeed, the plants used to make the wreaths were specifically chosen for their meaning and fragrance. But wreaths were not only for wall display; the garlands were also worn on the head as signs of honor and distinction.

Photo Credits

Photo Credits

Introduction

Page 6
Scala/Art Resource, NY

Page 7
(clockwise from top right)

TM & © 1998 Warner Bros.

© Michael W. Nelson/
UNIPHOTO

Archive Photos

Page 8
Colin Barker/
Tony Stone Images

Page 9
(clockwise from
middle right)

Kevin Horan/
Tony Stone Images

Brian Stablyk/
Tony Stone Images

© Charles Mann

Lunar New Year

Page 10
Manoj Shah/
Tony Stone Images

Page 11
(clockwise from top right)

Schafer & Hill/
Tony Stone Images

Joseph Pobereskin/
Tony Stone Images

Boltin Picture Library

Winter Sports

Page 12
© John Russell/
Network Aspen

Page 13
(clockwise from top right)

© John Russell/
Network Aspen

© John Russell/
Network Aspen

© John Russell/
Network Aspen

© Jeffrey Aaronson/
Network Aspen

Madam C. J. Walker

Page 14
A'Lelia Bundles/
Walker Family Collection

Page 15
(clockwise from top right)

A'Lelia Bundles/Walker
Family Collection/photogra-
phy Robert McClintock,
© PhotoAssist, Inc.

A'Lelia Bundles/
Walker Family Collection

A'Lelia Bundles/
Walker Family Collection

(background)

Photographs and Prints
Division, Schomburg Center
for Research in Black
Culture, The New York
Public Library, Astor, Lenox
and Tilden Foundations

U.S. Battleship *Maine*

Page 16
Library of Congress

Page 17
(clockwise from top right)

Ira Block, courtesy Key West
Art & Historical Society

Ira Block, courtesy U.S.
Naval Academy Museum

Ira Block

Archive Photos

(background)

The Granger Collection, NY

Flowering Trees

Page 18
Jerry Pavia

Page 19
(clockwise from
middle right)

© Michael A. Dirr

© Michael A. Dirr

© Michael A. Dirr

© Derek Fell

Alexander Calder

Page 20
UPI/Corbis-Bettmann

Page 21
(all including background)

© Tony Vaccaro

Cinco de Mayo

Page 22
Robert Daemmrich/
Tony Stone Images

Page 23
Robert Daemmrich/
UNIPHOTO

Robert Daemmrich/
Tony Stone Images

Robert Daemmrich/
Tony Stone Images

Sylvester & Tweety

Page 24
TM & © 1998 Warner Bros.

Page 25
(all including background)

TM & © 1998 Warner Bros.

Wisconsin Statehood

Page 26
© Zane Williams

Page 27
(clockwise from top right)

© Zane Williams

© Zane Williams

Zane Williams/
Tony Stone Images

© Zane Williams

(background)

© 1998 Brent Nicastro

Trans-Mississippi Reissue of 1898

Page 28
National Museum of
American Art, Washington,
DC/Art Resource, NY

Page 29
(clockwise from top right)

National Museum of
American Art, Washington,
DC/Art Resource, NY

Library of Congress/
PhotoAssist, Inc.

National Archives/
PhotoAssist, Inc.

(background)

Archive Photos

Berlin Airlift

Page 30
UPI/Corbis-Bettmann

Page 31
(all except background)

UPI/Corbis-Bettmann

(background)

National Archives/
PhotoAssist, Inc.

Folk Musicians

Page 32
Frank Driggs/Archive Photos

Page 33
(clockwise from top right)

Archive Photos

Frank Driggs/
Corbis-Bettmann

Bill Spilka/Archive Photos

Archive Photos

Gospel Singers

Page 34
UPI/Corbis-Bettmann

Page 35
(clockwise from top right)

Courtesy Music Division,
Library of Congress/
PhotoAssist, Inc.

Frank Driggs/Archive Photos

Charles Peterson/
Archive Photos

(background)

Courtesy Music Division,
Library of Congress/
PhotoAssist, Inc.

Stephen Vincent Benét

Page 36
Corbis-Bettmann

Page 37
(clockwise from top right)

Library of Congress, courtesy Thomas Benét/
PhotoAssist, Inc.

Library of Congress, courtesy Thomas Benét/
PhotoAssist, Inc.

UPI/Corbis-Bettmann

(background)

The Yale Collection of
American Literature,
Beinecke Rare Book and
Manuscript Library,
Yale University

Tropical Birds

Page 38
© Douglas Peebles/
Westlight

Page 39
(clockwise from top right)

Doug Wechsler/© VIREO

© Jack Jeffrey/PHOTO
RESOURCE HAWAII

© Robert A. Tyrrell

Alfred Hitchcock

Page 40
Photofest

Page 41
(both)

© Yousuf Karsh/Woodfin
Camp and Associates

Organ & Tissue Donation

Page 42
© 1998 Kevin Beebe/
Custom Medical Stock Photo

Page 43
(clockwise from top right)

UPI/Corbis-Bettmann

UPI/Corbis-Bettmann

Courtesy Coalition on Organ
& Tissue Donation

Bright Eyes

Page 44
© Renee Stockdale/
Animals Animals

Page 45
(clockwise from top right)

Ed Simpson/
Tony Stone Images

© Robert Pearcy/
Animals Animals

© Gerard Lacz/
Animals Animals

© Robert Maier/
Animals Animals

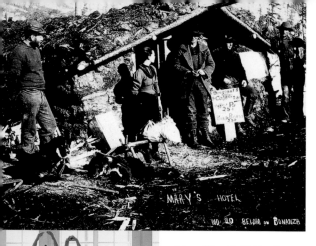

Klondike Gold Rush

Page 46
Archive Photos

Page 47
(clockwise from top right)
Archive Photos
Corbis-Bettmann
Corbis-Bettmann
Corbis-Bettmann

Four Centuries of American Art

Page 48
Art Resource, NY

Page 49
(clockwise from top right)
National Museum of American Art, Washington, DC/Art Resource, NY
National Museum of American Art, Washington, DC/Art Resource, NY
Bowdoin College Museum of Art, Brunswick, ME, gift of the Homer Family.
(background)
Image © 1998 PhotoDisc, Inc.

Ballet

Page 50
Erich Lessing/ Art Resource, NY

Page 51
(clockwise from top right)
Richard Clintsman/ Tony Stone Images
Charles Krebs/ Tony Stone Images
Lew Lause/UNIPHOTO
(background)
Jewish Museum/ Art Resource, NY

Space Discovery

Page 52
Attila Hejja/Mendola Ltd.

Page 53
(clockwise from top right)
Courtesy NASA/ Jet Propulsion Laboratory, California Institute of Technology
Image © 1998 PhotoDisc, Inc.
© 1954 Ivan Tors Production, Inc., courtesy NGM Consumer Products
Image © 1998 PhotoDisc, Inc.
(background)
Courtesy NASA/Jet Propulsion Laboratory, California Institute of Technology

Giving & Sharing: Philanthropy

Page 54
© Robert Rathe/FOLIO, Inc.

Page 55
(clockwise from middle right)
Reuters/Bruce Young/ Archive Photos
© Rob Crandall/FOLIO, Inc.
© Regis Lefebure/ FOLIO, Inc.
(background)
© Regis Lefebure/ FOLIO, Inc.

Madonna and Child

Page 56
The Andy Warhol Foundation, Inc./ Art Resource, NY

Page 57
(counterclockwise from top left)
Erich Lessing/ Art Resource, NY
Scala/Art Resource, NY
Erich Lessing/ Art Resource, NY
(background)
Don Morgan/Archive Photos

Holiday Wreaths

Page 58
Colonial Williamsburg Foundation

Page 59
(clockwise from top right)
Colonial Williamsburg Foundation
Ken McVey/ Tony Stone Images
© Charles Mann
© Sotographs/ Liaison International

Credits

Page 62
Zane Williams/ Tony Stone Images

Page 63
(top)
Robert Daemmrich/ Tony Stone Images
(bottom)
Archive Photos

Page 64
(counterclockwise from top left)
Archive Photos
Terry Vine/ Tony Stone Images
© Charles Mann
(background)
Image © 1998 PhotoDisc, Inc.

Acknowledgments

Special thanks to the individuals for their contributions to the production of this book.

The stamps and this book were produced by Stamp Services, United States Postal Service.

United States Postal Service
William J. Henderson
Postmaster General and Chief Executive Officer

Marvin Runyon
Former *Postmaster General*

Allen Kane
Chief Marketing Officer and Senior vice President

Azeezaly S. Jaffer
Executive Director, Stamp Services

Paul Ovchinnikoff
Print Supervision

Wanda Parks
Contract Administration

The Citizens' Stamp Advisory Committee

Manuel Vasquez
Project Manager

PhotoAssist, Inc.
Visual and historical research

Anne A. Jamison
Editor

Supon Design Group
Supon Phornirunlit
Art Director

Wayne Kurie
Managing Editor

Stephen Smith
Writer

Jason Drumheller and Sharisse Steber
Book Designers

Brent Almond, Andrew Berman, Ellen Kim, Jake Lefebure, Pum Mek-aroonreung, Jeanette Nelson, and Maria Sese Paul
Associate Designers